SNACKS FOR THE LOVE HUNGRY

SNACKS FOR THE LOVE HUNGRY

POEMS BY
VALERIE NIES

World Stage Press
Verse from the Village

World Stage Press
Verse from the Village

Snacks for the Love Hungry
© 2022, Valerie Nies
ISBN: 978-1-952952-44-9

First Edition, 2022

All rights reserved. No part of this publication may be reproduced, distributed, or transmitted in any form or by any means, including photocopying, recording, or other electronic or mechanical methods, without the prior written permission of the publisher, except in the case of brief quotations embodied in critical reviews and certain other noncommercial uses permitted by copyright law.

Printed in the United States of America

Edited by Laura Joy Phillips
Cover Design by Shiva Nosrati
Layout Design by Shiva Nosrati & Emily Anne Evans

For David Pink, who believed in my poetry before I did.

Table of Contents

PART I: SALTY BLACK LICORICE

3. Zillow > For Sale> Late 20th Century Redhead
4. He Asks About My Kinks
6. In This House
7. Ode to George W. Bush
9. Burnt Honey
10. Mourning Amnesia
12. Remnants on the Pool Table's Soft Felt
14. The Stuff that Keeps Me up at Night
15. Ode to a WeightWatchers Pioneer Who Loved Herself Enough to Defect
17. Sixth Date with a Widower Named Wax, Who Declared in His Dating Profile His Shit is Together
19. A Voicemail to Resentment
21. Despairathon
22. Ode to a Mansplainer
23. Late Stage Abyss Abecedarian
24. The God Grid Failed Texas
26. When I Die, What Happens To My Domains?

PART II: SNACKWELLS FAT-FREE DEVIL'S COOKIE CAKES

29. Bette Midler Dispenses Stray Advice During a Game of Playground Red Rover
30. Recollections from the Poet's Training Bra
32. Eddie Vedder Saved Me From A Cult
35. Graduating from Sundaes
36. I Drove a 1999 Yellow Ford Festiva
38. Stopping for Ayr in Rural North Dakota
39. Self-Portrait As A Ubiquitous Unkillable ZZ Plant

40. Marlboro Kool
41. Collecting Cash at the Phallic Factory
43. Home for Christmas
44. Mixed Messages
46. My Parents Almost Named Me Heather, A Ghazal
47. A Cherry That Chokes

PART III: FULL FAT CAPPUCCINO

51. The Red Hot Dogs from North Dakota
53. In Paris Where Even Work is Romantic
55. Ode to Woman Power a painting by Austrian artist Maria Lassnig, who Grew Into New York City circa 1979 Maria Lassnig
56. Attempting to Accelerate Progress
58. Four Enlightened Americans Travel to Antigua, Guatemala to Build a House and Visit Ruins
60. Mates versus Mates
61. The Privilege of Never Having to Go Home
62. An Endless Driving Sestina
64. Traveling During a Global Pandemic
65. Mexico City is Sinking

PART IV: 100-CALORIE PACK

69. Snacks for the Love Hungry
71. Five Stages of Grief
72. If I'd Put My Clothes Back On And Left Your Bedroom
74. Ode to Dewalt
75. 12 Mourning Habits for a Productive Sorrow
76. Hanging Your Name on the Wall
78. Single Women Can't Stop Buying Shit
79. An Algorithm of Imagined Future Horrors

81. Nocturnal Intersection
82. A Golden Shovel for the Widower Named Wax
83. In Care of Lalo

PART V: TRAIL MIX

87. A Plea from the Poet's Unopened Mail
89. It Took Me 39 Years
90. Earth Has Attachment Issues
91. To the Professor Who First Assigned Me The Love Song of J. Alfred Prufrock
93. Something that Makes his Voice Creak
94. A Night Shift Worker to the Poet
95. Haiku to My Imaginary Friend Marc Maron
96. My Frenemy, the Super Plus Tampon
97. What I Really Hear When He Says We Are "Just Hanging Out"
98. Henry Winkler Gives Me Permission to Quit Therapy
100. My Immune System Ignites a Forest Fire On My Face, aka a Pandemic Pantoum
101. A Day's Worth of Net Losses & Gains, April 16, 2021
102. Last Night, My Pothos Plant
103. First Date with Herman Melville Reincarnated
104. The Spigot Fairy
106. To the Man I Dated Who Thought Sunsets were Overrated
107. Happy Meal Hours
108. The White Picket Promise

111. Acknowledgments

PART I

SALTY BLACK LICORICE

ZILLOW > FOR SALE > LATE 20TH CENTURY REDHEAD

Built in the late 70s / Eclectic / Four feet eleven inches tall, but plenty of storage with built-in shame shelves / Newly renovated backbone / A mouth full of knives / Ears that love to hear a baritone voice through the wall of a man's chest / Swivel neck, perfect for looking backwards / Vintage shoulders, tight from not yet knowing work-life balance / Lungs that often audibly sigh / Pompous elbows to hide small psoriasis patch / Belly that plumps like a restuffed feather pillow after every *this isn't working* out / Thick thighs you will grow to love / Wild toes that often stub themselves / Not winterized / A superb choice for the reincarnated soul who seeks a cosmos of validation / Warning: Seller has pattern of pulling her listing once others express interest.

HE ASKS ABOUT MY KINKS

Because I feel naked
during these conversations, I start small,
with the lights turned off. Tell him I like my hair pulled.
He nods. Tell him I like dirty talk: *Spank
me, daddy. Lick my geode.*

And then what? he asks.
Because he has a sister and a Planned Parenthood
bumper sticker on his fridge, I reveal fantasies I've never said
aloud, like what really rocks my clam is going
to the Thai restaurant on South First

with a 33-year-old video editor named Jeremy
and not having to text my girlfriends
my location *in case I die*. What pinches
my nipples is getting caught with my legs
hugging his face in the middle

of a downtown avenue under streetlamps,
turned on bright for once to save women instead
of dimmed to save the city a few bucks. What wets
my carpet is being blindfolded with a *Future
is Female* t-shirt while reruns of a sitcom

about a peppy blond bureaucrat who runs
for office in Indiana air during the *Law and Order: SVU* slot
because there are no more stories
of jealous husbands prying open their wives'
skulls with happily never afters.

Because the last time I had sex I said *yes*,
not because I wanted to, but because my boyfriend's
eyes said *I deserve this* and *you belong
to me,* and I didn't want a story I'd
have to keep in the back

of my nightstand like a velvet satchel
of trauma. I'd rather pull out
a hot pink vibrator than a hot pink taser. It would be so hot
to make a man my cuckold. Except instead of watching me fuck
another guy, he's watching me watch edgy, white male filmmakers

write something *they* know instead
of yet another fetishized rape scene, and then maybe
I tickle his ear and whisper: *One in six women, or maybe
it's four?* until he begs me to stop. *Stop. STOP.
I have nieces.*

Like that's his safe word.

IN THIS HOUSE

we believe Tom Brady
will play football forever.
We believe in crisp white linen

buttoned-down family photos pulled
up with bootstrapped drycleaning privilege.
We believe in naming

our kids Gideon and Stella
and decorating their rooms with elephant-print
teepees. We believe in building up

an ultraposh sustainably sourced meat market
while tearing down the family
carnicería. We believe in living, laughing,

and loving our leaf blowers. We believe in reclaiming
wood, tinned fish, Basquiat's ideas,
and this neighborhood as our own.

We believe in hiding insecurities
underneath pendant lights
that illuminate our farmhouse

dining room tables, shiplapping
banality behind vases of bleached
blond stalks of wheat. We believe in Whole30,

xeriscaped dog parks, and manifest destinying
yoga. We believe in screaming
into our wine o'clock pillows

when we see the rising
property taxes,
we don't believe we caused.

We believe
in paying our accountants
to get us out of paying.

ODE TO GEORGE W. BUSH

In the 90s, my skin was an oily
patch of puberty. Tender pink bumps, landmines
of angst. Treatment involved scooping lather-y liquids armed
for the battleground of hormonal skin. A greasy cream
called Noxzema from a navy blue tub, noxious, chemical
cleanser, like Pine-Sol for my face. Made in Ocean City, Maryland,
owned by a company called Unilever. A lever is a rigid
bar resting on a pivot, used to help move a firmly fixed load
with one end when pressure is applied to the other. Like my fingertips
pressing against either side of a zit to pop it.

After the Noxzema bath, I'd yellowcake
a cotton ball of a tingly astringent across my pores.
Made in the USA, a product called Sea Breeze,
like if the wind picked up a whiff from a sea tanker
leaking Agent Orange.

I'd coat my raw face in gummy Clearasil,
an ointment invented during the second era
of the military industrial complex by a mad
chemist in White Plains, New York.
For tender pubescent faces, this sadist
mixed benzoyl peroxide to peel skin like beef jerky,
with sulfur to redden and pillage
pores, and salicylic acid to melt
epidermis like napalm.

                              And then George Bush senior signed NAFTA.

And Bill Clinton said *globalization is the economic equivalent of a force of nature, like water* that adolescents wash their faces with twice a day.

            And George W. Bush signed the U.S.-Korea Free Trade Agreement
so Sephora's shelves could fill with Korean
skincare products and our faces could finally sigh in peace.

                              This asshole who started a made-up war on
                                terror, waterboarded prisoners, and had
                                   a shoe thrown at him, is the same
                                                                authority

responsible for my access to dewy sheet masks,
soft linen soaked in in aloe,
warm moisturizing serums,
cool jade to roll under my puffy eyes.
Well. I'm reluctant to say it, but:
                    mission accomplished.

BURNT HONEY

My sister, a brunette
giraffe whose skin pops against
a field of dandelions.

I was a short squirrel chatting,
begging her to tell me how the
Earth could spin while spinning.

When I told my sister
to stop tickling me,
she tickled me more.

When I asked my sister about tampons,
she told me to read the directions
on the box. When I asked my sister

for movie suggestions the first time
I invited Paul Dillard over, she said
A Clockwork Orange, so we made out

during a rape scene. I tacked
a photo on my silver fridge. Of us. When she was eight
and I was five. We are frosting

burnt honey
cookies at an avocado-
colored dining room table,

my mother's grandfather clock towering
behind us—the grandfather clock
my sister asked me how she should

ask our mother to one day give her.
Two tall things in a house belong together.
I said, *Sweetly. Not big and demanding.*

Like the bass note chime that rings
from the clock in my living room, which I pull
out a ladder to dust each spring.

MOURNING AMNESIA

My tabby cat's orange scruff grows
back like dandelion cotton
after this last operation,
tickling my hand.

Reminds me of the stubble dust
on my grandfather's cheeks, sandpapering
my face when we would say goodbye
after Easter or Thanksgiving visits,

when I was a huggable, wee creature
inventing worlds underneath
the table, personifying old-timey toys
my mother once played

with when she was my age:
dancing green and blue jacks,
well-postured wooden blocks,
a bouffant Barbie with a bent leg.

Above me, the adults played pinochle
and conversational tug o' war
over decaf coffee. Later,
when I was teenager, I hated these visits.

Rolled my eyes listening to my uncles' baritone voices
complain about the price of soybeans,
my grandfather gruff about the cards or crops,
half in German incomprehensible to my impatient

inner squirrel while grandma chimed
does anyone want more cheese or another beer?
I'd frost my eyes toward my parents, raise
my yellow-Swatched wrist. I never learned to play

cards while my grandfather was living.
Now, I yearn to be dealt back
into a game, where I am conscious,
where all the cats my grandfather

loved, and I love, live forever,
where droughts are never,
where the only wounds
on inner children

are skinned knees
that crust over with courage,
where, like my grandfather said the last
time I saw him

before, the I last saw him,
I could be elected governor
if I wanted,
and my first rules of order

would be to unbend
every broken Barbie,
pollute oceans with abalone shells,
strip suburbia of strip malls,

and give myself mourning amnesia.
So that I could forget
that with every loss,
I experience every loss.

REMNANTS ON THE POOL TABLE'S SOFT FELT

Billiards became popular in the 15th century among the French nobility
    and in my friend Carrie's basement around 10th grade, when we'd drink
Hot Damn and sing along to Garbage. Pool playing is a rom-com shortcut

    to reveal hot starlets as carefree women undemanding of their leading men.
A pool-playing chick hooks up her TV herself and enjoys
    paying for BBQ after her label-less beau shows up 47 minutes late

for their Saturday date. When I lean over a pool table, it's more struggle
    than sexy. Perhaps because I'm short. Like this video I once saw of a turtle attempting
to climb steps. Why is a turtle even near stairs? Grasping

    for things that don't make sense for its life path?
A turtle prefers ponds and grass, but here's this reptile YouTube star
    trying to surmount a Berber-covered split-level. Just stop.

But sometimes, it takes a lot of evidence to determine
    what is or is not ours. I was never good at playing pool in bars,
though I excelled at drinking in bars and at parties and on my patio alone

    with my cat, chain-smoking, scrolling through Facebook to spy enviously
on other people's purposeful lives, which mine was not. I drank
    like this for years before someone, or many people, pointed out buying six

packs of Coors Light from Chevron, drinking five and surrendering
    the sixth down the sink, vowing to stop forever, wasn't healthy.
But before this, in my early 20s, surrounded by unhealthy,

I'd play pool at Midwestern bars named Sidelines and Sports Bar,
    even though I was the least sporty person. Stubbled men in hockey jerseys
and hunting camo, blond women with fake tans named Cammy chalked up

    cues, the way fawns know how to walk straight from the womb. Shoot
and click, followed by striped or solid spheres rhythmically rolling
    toward a pocket, the sound of upstairs neighbors moving furniture. Not me.

I looked like a bad improviser, never knowing how much chalk was too much.
    But not liking pool is not an option where I grew up. Like ice fishing and marrying
too young and drenching salads in mayonnaise—it's a heartland prerequisite.

My hands never knew how to grip the pool stick with control, stuttering uneven
as it fumbled toward a scratched cue ball. That part felt familiar—pointing at things I
    thought were my destiny. Chalk dust on hands. An immediate mistake. Wanting

to wash it off right away. My fingers, already so end-of-November dry.
    On that one night, I don't remember if I actually played pool, or just watched.
I remember flirting with the guy from high school I never talked to but now, five years

    later on Thanksgiving break, had so much in common with: writing, good hair, green
parkas with furry hoods. I remember anger at my boyfriend for staying home, being
    handed tall beers, someone driving us in a Toyota or Lexus. The next morning,

I saw white handprints on my stretchy black New York & Company blouse spread
    on my bedroom floor beside a condom wrapper that told me one of two stories:
I'd cheated on the boyfriend for whom my 23-year-old infant heart wanted

    to marry too young and make bowls of mayo salads. Or, the other one—
that for years I called a *gray area* to counselors and over coffees
    with women who possessed their own gray areas.

It's easier. Not too harsh. A mirage. Remnants
    outlined on the pool table's soft felt, an ignorable crayon, the inside
of my cat's ears, an emptied but unwashed ashtray, the entire sky of San Francisco.

THE STUFF THAT KEEPS ME UP AT NIGHT

Would buying a Roomba help me pick up the stacks of paper on my floor?
What happened to the owners of the orphaned socks and sneakers I see on sidewalks
I stroll past in my neighborhood?
My desire for marriage and his desire to bone all the women he fears.
Trader Joe's unnecessary plastic packaging on red peppers.
Why is family therapy for all not a thing?

Do you want kids?

The brown bananas meditating on my counter.
One day I will adopt a gentle orange tabby
like the one from four blocks down.
Am I alone causing the Pacific
Ocean trash vortex?
My thyroid gland's apathy, and my belly's
zeal for growth.

Is it okay if I call you Val?

All my privilege.
No one knows the male equivalent for the word misogyny.

Will my gray tabby cat die because I doted on the neighbor's ginger cat?

How tall are you?
The chorus to "Cover Me in Sunshine."
Does everyone else feel perpetually 17 years old?

There is no male counterpart for the word femicide.

ODE TO A WEIGHTWATCHERS PIONEER WHO LOVED HERSELF ENOUGH TO DEFECT

Evelyn Lovie, my father's mother,
proprietor of guilt over her unswept kitchen,
a shiny white Casio keyboard she used to play
"When the Saints Go Marching

In," and crochet hooks I could never
grip. A WeightWatchers pioneer.
Before points and tracking macros,
she made her own

sugar-free ketchup.
Because she gave a fuck.
But later, she displayed
fake flowers in the beds curbing

her home. Because she did not
give a fuck. Because she grew
into her name, an affirmation. She graveled
hymns in church choirs, flaunted

at least one chipped nail, and at some point
housed a whole pantry of Fiddle Faddle caramel corn.
When I was eight, and my summer
cousins frenzied fried chicken and potato salad

from the kitchen, I—an only child
unaccustomed to the chaos of yelling
hands—read books, sympathized with
unfortunate gray-chinned dogs, feared choking

on chicken bones and not being related
to my dodgeball family. Evelyn Lovie endowed
me as softhearted. She who was gentle-spoken,
wrinkle-elbowed, and,

in the end, close-
curtain-brained Evelyn Lovie
saw me like I could never:
lovely.

SIXTH DATE WITH A WIDOWER NAMED WAX WHO DECLARED IN HIS DATING PROFILE HIS SHIT IS TOGETHER

It takes you a month
of text exchanges, six dinners,
five phone conversations, four frozen desserts,
three makeout sessions,
two strolls around a lake
and one sunset
for you tell me you'd have preferred to get to know
each other over after-dinner drinks,
rather than after-dinner gelato,
but you didn't want to make
me uncomfortable by suggesting
a bar.

The only thing
that makes me uncomfortable
is when a crepe-y-skinned man who fails
to wear sunblock makes a decision for me
about *my* health. When a 49-year-old who feasts
on three Taco Bell cheesy rollups at 9pm on a Tuesday thinks he knows
what's best for me. When a man who waxes
poetic about us sharing
the same birthday,
both liking Wu Chow's Szechuan string beans
and streaming LA radio stations as signs
we're meant to be together,
doesn't read reality when I say I'm sober,
can't have kids, have never been, nor ever want
to go water skiing. The only
thing that makes me uncomfortable is
when a man who suggests a 14-dollar breakfast
is too expensive then blows up
$90 on fireworks thinks he knows how my life
should be managed. When a man who eats two afternoon
edibles to escape his own grief
while staining the deck on the gentrified condo
he bought with his dead

wife, which he can no longer afford,
wants to protect me
from assumed discomfort
without asking first how I feel.

        Well let me tell you:
        I climbed up 12 steps
        of drunk dials
        going on nine years ago,
        tilled hangover headaches into lotus blossoms,
        while drinking lukewarm Folgers
        from styrofoam cups in church basements. Swallowed honest
        vitamins, nourished my past with forgiveness,
        abstained from booze at funerals and weddings,
        through breakups and beginnings,
        through feasts and fires, four years of Trump,
        sitting alone, staring at my phone for months
        during a global pandemic and somehow you think sizzling
        across from you on a Saturday night, feelin sexy
        in sleek black, sipping sparkling water, dining on seafood
        and batting eyelashes, is gonna make me relapse?

        You think you know me after a month
        of too much investment too quickly,
        four podcast recommendations about grief,
        three future promises to take me dinner at La Condesa,
        to the San Antonio Museum of Art, to the skate park,
        two shared love languages, and one last
        conversation where I discover
        you do not know definitions for the words
        feminist or hysterectomy, think the movie *Crash*
        deserved its Oscar, define weekly cannabis
        use as Thursday through Sunday,
        maybe, sometimes, Wednesdays too,
        which might be too much haze
        to describe yourself as authentic,
        but could be the exact right amount of weed
        to wonder if *you* might feel uncomfortable hanging with a sober girl.

My shit is together.

A VOICEMAIL TO RESENTMENT

Hey—
If you could call
me back, I'd
appreciate it.
Because if you don't,
all I'm left with is that
bitch Fear
who's like a memo
from God
telling me to trust.

And we both know that guy's unreliable.
Whenever he does communicate, it's so cryptic.
A vision of Jesus' face
in someone's toast?
C'mon.

I'm never certain
if he or she or whatever is sending a message,
or if I'm leaning into the literature-loving,
Jungian part of myself that finds symbolism
in anything: a conversation
at Trader Joe's with a friend who's moving to LA,
where I've debated relocating for years
to pursue all those clichés, and she says,
Maybe you'll know if you want it, when you want it.
And then, as soon as she leaves with her baby bananas
and bouquet of gerbera daisies, a Joe Jackson song
plays on the sound system,
the one that plays in every grocery store:
"You Can't Get What You Want ('til you know
what you want)." Over and over,
that one statement is the entire song.

And then I stop at the sample station
to try a Tuscan salami and Danish cheese
a week before I'm supposed to take my first solo trip

to Florence and Copenhagen, which
I've worst-case scenario'd for four months
since I bought the ticket off Scott's Cheap Flights.

And what's with the feathers,
anyway? When I see them on the ground
 is that God talking?
To me?
Or are there just too many damn
grackles in this city?
Blessed with parking lots of pizza crust,
those damn birds never worry
about having enough.

DESPAIRATHON

You've spent a lifetime training
for this. Reach into your past-
hat, pull out a white rabbit of lost
lipsticks, dead pets, and melancholia
to remind yourself when your husband
leaves after 33 years of marriage
to fuck his jiu-jitsu instructor
but returns weekly
to the house
you still share
to blow leaves off the driveway.

ODE TO A MANSPLAINER

Your lips, a white horse
rescuing damsels from dangerous
silence, condescending kittens out of trees.
Well-intentioned tidbits,
shielding me from the street-side
of the sidewalk.
Adjacent to me at the sushi bar, your mouth
runneth over with syllables explaining
what I already know—
Steely Dan was named after a sex toy—
other times, what I may not even care about—
*the Austrian economic school contraposes
egalitarian tenets of objective value—*
and sometimes in the grocery store coffee aisle, pointing
out what I already said, now in your own words:
heavier rainfall sweetens the beans.

Well, actually,
it is a fact men gift us:
twenty-five percent more
words in work meetings than women.
Generous verbosity. On dates, you interrupt
doors for me. Slay dragons with your opinion.
Where would I be if you hadn't told
me Bernanke destroyed the American dollar,
Hillary was a technocrat, marriage is capitalist,
pine is the best wood to whittle a spoon,
or that I should avoid eating lectins?

So smooth is your speech, like my freshly
exfoliated lips, that I wish you would shut up
and kiss instead of giving an oral history
on the discography of Guided By Voices.
Chivalry isn't dead until a man tells a woman so.

Watch the poem here:

LATE STAGE ABYSS ABECEDARIAN

Abyss: a word I divested from poems about grief.
Because what the hell does it mean?
Can you sit inside an abyss?
Drive to an abyss? Where does it
exist? Where does the word come
from? Its origin,
Greek: *abyssos*, meaning bottomless.
How did that become negative?
If a bottomless pot of coffee is morning
jubilation, why does a bottomless pit feel like moaning
knives? And can I buy something to make it stop?
Longing quenched with
materialism. *Abyssinia*, an empire containing one of the only
nations in Africa that was never colonized in an abyss
of abuse. We could shower the world in
Pepto Bismal, and it still wouldn't
quell the abysmal
returns on investment of a
society soaked in late stage
tyrannical capitalism,
unfair distribution unfolding at cardboard intersections,
video ads targeting us
with our own words, profiting off
xenophobia, so Amazon kings can invest in high-
yield dividend stocks. The abyss sits in a mountain where a billionaire
zealot banks his clock.

THE GOD GRID FAILED TEXAS

In a state cinched at the waist
with a belt made from Bibles,
God was too angry to keep the power
on, they said.

Poseidon came back from Mexico
with Giardia and gave it to the Pisces fish who froze
swimming up the pipes.

Edesia, who loved to eat
and eat and eat, left only stray
spinach leaves at the corner Fresh Plus, so Scarcity,
 goddess   of nothing
and fewer, could shine
minimalism—

                              or that's what I heard from Mercury
                              next door.

Prometheus took a vacation, then murdered
an 11-year-old immigrant in his bed after playing in the snow
for the first time that day.

Vayu and Marzanna made hard love in a sacred
live oak tree to keep warm,
then blew down the branches, which snapped
a Prius, but blessed
some guilty fool with heat for the night.

And on the seventh day,
when everyone was tired and ready to go home,
the Capricorn sea-goat showed up with a keg to flood
our spirits.

For a week, the gods played poker and smoked cigars,
like bachelor party savages, the men told us,
while neighbors collected twigs and melted
snow for toilet tanks.

The men who once hung billboards praising
Jesus is Alive along highways, serpentining
cotton fields, deserts, hills, coastal bends, oil
wells, and panhandle plains said this while they took shits
in the yards they landscaped with new gold.

WHEN I DIE, WHAT HAPPENS TO MY DOMAINS?

The ones purchased years ago after nights of drinking—
brilliant ideas: the unrealized satirical recipe site, the aborted
vintage resale shop, the almost-
film production company?

AmateurFoodiePorn.com, I'm sorry.
MyNanasCloset.com, I apologize.
NeuroticaProductions.com, forgive me.
I assume you're all sitting in group therapy, healing
emotional wounds because I was so unavailable.

When I die, what happens to the domains
I purchased after sunny spurts of creative optimism:
the never-followed-through sobriety travel blog, the imposter-syndromed
editing school, the abandoned podcast?

To SoberSojourns.com, I leave
my AA chips and a full passport. To OneHundredProof.com, I leave
Roget's Thesaurus and my blue blocker glasses.
To HelpWanted.com, I leave
what I've read from every self-help book I own:
the first three chapters.

To be split among you equally:
my perfectionism. May I release
my tight grip of it in death.

PART II

SNACKWELL'S FAT-FREE DEVIL'S COOKIE CAKES

BETTE MIDLER DISPENSES STRAY ADVICE DURING A GAME OF PLAYGROUND RED ROVER

Hold tight, Bette says prancing behind me and the girl whose hand folds into mine. The game is to prevent the other team's players from breaking through our fence of six-year-old arms. But I'm cursed with the weakness of a wavy, wacky inflatable tube man. A third kid cracks through my barrier. A pattern. Every time this happens, the opposing team snatches one of our strong kids, and I'm met with sneers from the recess oligarchy—future one percenters and corrupt dictators, I imagine. Bette says *Ah well. You're good at other things.* I want to ask "What?" but this seems audacious and, after all, I'm from the Midwest. Bette is Audacious with a capital A. As an actor, she assumes we all always want to hear about ourselves, because she says, *You're good at making people laugh,* which sounds like a key shifting into place the first time you unlock the door of a new apartment decorated in promises. Nothing is more satisfying, and I can say that because, honey, I've had an album go triple platinum. The other team sends more rovers to my weak arm. Our team depletes. Just me and the girl whose hand folds into mine. *Hold tight. You're in it together* Bette says. *I know it's hard, but trust is more important than running fast on playgrounds, or even winning a Tony. In the future, you'll excel at grasping too hard. For instance, the girl whose hand you're holding is named Betsy Gohl. She'll become your best friend this year, until her dad's job relocates their family to a Denver suburb. You'll be crushed until third grade. That betrayal will squat in your nervous system and only clear after a deep session of EMDR in your thirties.* Fascinating, but irrelevant. What I really want to know is the best way to find approval on competitive playgrounds. Bette says *People love Vegas, but I personally despise it. I was turned down for Sister Act, and that's okay. It wasn't meant for me. Instead, I got to wear polka dots and play two versions of myself in Big Business. Even better.* "What else should know?" I ask. *Big oil is trash. Recycling isn't real* she says. *Put your efforts into composting. Leave your hometown. Oh, and always call yourself Divine.*

RECOLLECTIONS FROM THE POET'S TRAINING BRA

Before me,
you dropped out of
ballet class, tired
from slouching, hiding what
the plié-ing tweens already knew:
you had boobs. Evidenced by your
fourth grade Disneyland vacation photos—
your torso whooping, *Hey look! I'm a woman.*
You needed me for at least a year before finally allowing
your mother to take you shopping to find me, frill-free, flopping
on a rack in a fluorescent-lit Sears. I trained you for skills you'd never need:
reconciling unnecessary dangling straps no mature version of me ever possessed.
Bury them in the polyester utilitarian uni-cup? Or cut them off and cross your fingers
your shoulders would never change sizes? I hazed you. Preparation for a lifetime wondering
whether anything you were supposed to wear or do or prove or be as a woman had any point.

I tried to keep you secure. Failed when that grown-up driving a vintage mustard Chevy pulled up beside your Huffy, poked his head out the window to say *nice tits* on your way to the park to hang with Monica Magnison, proprietor of the right currency: dishwater-blond spiral perm, lake cabin, ideal-sized thighs, and a flat chest. For at least one day, owning me made you an expert to Monica's mom who, while you picked black olives off pizza casserole in her dining room, asked, "Where does your mother buy your training bras?" For once, it was Monica who left the table, embarrassed, foreshadowing the sixth grade when her underlings demanded you find a new lunch spot, leaving you standing alone, protruding above the cafeteria plane like conspicuous developments shaping a baggy cotton t-shirt. Many friends, then two body parts, then one you. A first lesson in owning the parts of yourself you resist.

EDDIE VEDDER SAVED ME FROM A CULT

Not one of those fun tantric sex ones, either.
No. I was 14 years old when lured inside a temple
of dogs, acceptance-seeking adolescents

who hadn't yet discovered drugs,
so sought instead nirvana
at a Pentecostal church. This was the year of fitting in

Guess Jeans, eating fat-free Yoplait, gossiping
on the band room steps, and comparing
my thighs to those of every Alice in crash diet

chains. The year of privately practicing pentatonic
scales on my used Ovation with the amp turned low.
This was the year I, a girl

who had never been kissed, signed a red
index card, vowing to abstain
from sex until marriage,

even though all I wanted
was to bone every Josh who made up the hormone
of Nordic blond teenage boys tambourining

on stage in a church basement with sounds, rock 'n' roll
adjacent. Tall boy arms cradled
a bass, stocky Viking slouched at a trap set, smacking

drumsticks, and a bandana-wearing singer's hands caressed
a Stratocaster I wished were my face.
Every Wednesday night I exalted

this junior high temptation trinity. Crossed
my fingers I might flirt, prayed I'd find the right
words to make just one Josh notice

me, become my boyfriend, take to me the movies
where we could speak in tongues.
And if it was not God's will

for me to experience love, holy mother
of Mary Janes, could I at least possess
the same confidence as adolescent boys in a Christian band?

Who, even after strumming a wrong
chord or missing a beat, still smiled at the audience, a flock
of meat puppets. Instead, I meekly

played Led Zeppelin in my parents' basement,
an empty soundgarden. In the nine months I attended youth
group, I played "Enter Sandman" 99 times but spoke to only one male:

Pastor Bill, a 30 year-old who had moved to my hometown
in North Dakota from Seattle to save confused
Midwestern teenagers. To Pastor Bill, grunge rock Mecca

was Babylon and Eddie Vedder, Satan's minion. To prove
my devotion to God, he requested I hand over my CDs as an offering.
Sacrificial lambs. Like Job, I deliberated.

Listened to *Animal* searching for blasphemy.
Every riff, a revelation.
Listened to DC Talk, gifted from the pastor,

searching for redemption.
If indie rock is so evil,
why was it the only thing that made me feel alive?

If God were so great,
heavens to Betsy,
why did he suck

so hard at lyrics?
Like attempting to learn the solo from "Free
Bird," I became bored with church, forsook

Pastor Bill and the chorus of Joshes,
surrendered my hot pink Lisa Frank-styled teen Bible for rock 'n'
roll, drugs, and sex, which entered my life

in that order. Substituted writing vows of abstinence
in my teens for writing down my number in my twenties
on beverage napkins in bars with jukeboxes

singing "Yellow Ledbetter," turning to troubled musicians
I'd later have premarital sex with
because I finally found a compelling

opening line: Let me tell you the
story of how Eddie Vedder saved
me from a cult.

GRADUATING FROM SUNDAES

Somewhere
in south Bismarck on some
November day, at some girlfriend's
boyfriend's unseen older brother's
trailer house, six of us sugar-speed
sit on a smashed velour couch.
Electricity turned off, two warm
Schlitz beers buzzing
from a dark refrigerator, glide
down my smooth tulip
throat, split my brain into hot
fudge and freeze,
candying conversation.
Confidence sprinkled
on me for the first time,
flirting with maraschino cherry-
faced boys, who act
like they are men,
laughing in waves,
like mountains and valleys
of whipped cream.

I DROVE A 1991 YELLOW FORD FESTIVA

fueled with Grateful Dead
bumper stickers, code
to inform everyone in Bismarck,
my town of 60,000,
I was down to get high.

An economy-sized two-door,
cozy like a Champion hoodie,
the 1997 equivalent of a weighted blanket,
a suitcase of CDs on the passenger seat
and a compass pointing to all the fun
ways to avoid feeling.
All I knew was every lyric
to *Exile in Guyville*.
We could go anywhere.

A Sublime engine covered in Led Zeppelin
metal floating on top of Nine Inch Nails wheels.
Quilted tan seat covers branded in Marlboro Light
burns transported me from my parents' house
to community college metal desks,
from waitressing at The Woodhouse
to parties after each shift with older guys named Monte.

Free-falling down a winding cottonwood-lined River Road
with Tom Petty and my boyfriend Dave
whose love language was filling the hatchback
with a subwoofer and Alpine
amp. My love language back:
weaving him hemp necklaces with beads of unavailability.

To 6th Street and Avenue E,
where long-haired Yvonne lived
in a sunny cottage decorated in macrame
and vintage mushroom knickknacks.
After the sun set, it was carpeted
in drugs brought by a young man with a suitcase from Bakersfield.

Like an unnecessary interlude from a Smashing
Pumpkins song, it stayed dark.
Yvonne got pregnant with a drug dealer's baby.
At 19, I told a friend she should get an abortion.
She didn't. Today I still carry my word shame,
my blackout holier-than-thou hometown
shame. I'd love to say I left because I was brave,
because I knew the roads only led to meth
or marriage, but it was my mistakes that fueled me.

All I knew was I couldn't go anywhere
unless I got the hell out.

STOPPING FOR AYR IN RURAL NORTH DAKOTA

We pass a small town on I-29 surrounded in myth.
Inside the church, a friend
of a friend once heard, the crucifix glows red.

We can't decide if that's a good
or bad thing,
but stop. After all, we too are searching

and striving to breathe. In
quest
of awe
and breakfast. We find a dark,

dusty cafe, grocery store, post-office-slash-
town-hall in one lonely
building, with a woman, Rosie, suffocating.

Frying eggs
with sixty-year-old arthritic hands.
The church was closed, but the eggs: perfect, ambrosial.

SELF-PORTRAIT AS A UBIQUITOUS, UNKILLABLE HOUSEPLANT

A ZZ plant, I was at 15.
A slow grower who wanted to perform soliloquies
on windowsills, instead loitered
in the corner of a nail salon, flourishing in neglect.

An accent. The funny one. The independent one.
Attention would have withered
shy me. But behind curtains in shaded parking lots,
gnarly shoots sprouted from my core.

Sturdy leaves too stubborn
to drop. Even yellowed, came back
flipping off photosynthesis. Overlooked
in indirect light until years

later, I matured
into a focal point,
consuming living rooms,
learning there is no single right

radiance to shine in. My toxic
parts transformed into praise,
propagating life
in even the driest soil.

Like a recovering alcoholic
who opens a rehab,
giving oxygen
to entire rooms.

MARLBORO KOOL

You were what
I wanted to be:
long-legged,
Virginia Slim.
The Merit
keeping me and
the lead singer
at the party
stuck together
outside in conversation.
A meal's epilogue.
Friend to my war-fighting
grandfathers'
American Spirits.
Suicide's training
wheels. Cough
that broke
the Camel's
back. Always
burning at
one end.

COLLECTING CASH AT THE PHALLIC FACTORY

It's the summer before my sophomore year in college
and I'm sheathed in blue-collared testosterone eyes
inside a cement cube. A factory
of men who smell like cigarettes, toxic citrus
GOJO hand soap, and no means yes. I work
twelve-hour days on an assembly line
in August heat alongside stubbly men
who think I'm there for them

and not the 16 bucks an hour I will save
to pay my living expenses in the fall
at a state university where I will write essays
about Mary Wollstonecraft and her *Vindication on the Rights
of Women* to work beside men equally, putting parts
together for excavation equipment.
Pistons and heads and seals and shafts
to build masculine mechanical dinosaurs that bore
holes in dirt, penetrate
earth for urban development.

Men who drive big-wheeled trucks silhouetted
in window decals of impossibly busty women
with extreme nipples
and cartoon hair with ends
that never split.

I hide
myself in dialogue. Tell the men *I love
Black Sabbath, I love the sabbath*,
start every sentence with *my boyfriend*.
My boyfriend lifts weights at the gym too.
My boyfriend likes when I wear a ponytail.
My boyfriend bought me pepper spray.

A short one chases me with a spray bottle
to splash water on my chest, like we are in an
episode of *Three's Company*. I hide
myself in the baggiest, cotton T-shirts so the men

will think I am one of them, forget they thought
I'm here to tempt them from their wives or temper
their loneliness from the wives who left them.

Tell them to turn up the volume
I love The Cars I say as they drool and watch me
shove rods inside hydraulic cylinders. They fantasize
I am pushing *them* into some kind of metal fleshlight.

Hide myself in kindness and gifts, pull out
from my Igloo cooler at lunch by the lockers
confidence and candy: Twizzlers and Kit Kats
to distract them. Like throwing bread at ducks,
until one day, a tall one corners me, tells me he wants to watch me
suck on a lollipop, whip licorice with my tongue,
choke on chocolate.

And, I'd love to say I called HR, or
that I quit my job, but I did neither.
And I could give you a file cabinet of excuses:
it was 1999, my dad worked at the same plant,
I didn't want to find out who's side he'd take, all
the women who came before me had it worse,
I didn't know I could find mentors in the generation
after mine, the younger women who would not
put up with, would not fumble in hot rage, would not
boys will be boys away their comfort, would not stay silent,
would not.

HOME FOR CHRISTMAS

We peel potatoes over the sink
and she vents about my father.

All he does is watch TV.
Every Sunday, NASCAR
races, she says.
He never talks to me.

He's nicknamed me.
Calls me Bertha
every time I forget something,
or if we're going out and I take too long getting dressed.

Well, I smirk,
you do act like
Grandma sometimes.

What's funny about that?
What if your husband were to call you by my name?

MIXED MESSAGES

After I tell two ninth graders to fuck off
for calling me fat outside Claire's Boutique,
my mother says, *You're 13! That language
is not becoming!* I think I am Lenny Bruce.
Or at least Christian Slater in that movie
where his character thinks he's Lenny Bruce.
My dagger tongue brings me a year's worth
of bully torture in junior high hallways.

An adolescence of eff bombs, tantrums
and obscene soliloquies delivered to undeserving
family members, then in adulthood to AT&T customer service reps,
Trader Joe's parking lot idiots,
perplexed lovers, line cutters,
the cashier at the laundromat
with the washing machine that rips me off $1.75.
They say a watched pot never boils,
but a pot ignored pouts, seethes,
severs connection.

But also: My neighbors thank me,
a four-foot-eleven superhero,
because the mailboxes are finally fixed
after I call the post office each day,
and at 33 I grow blessed
to never again have bad sex
because assertiveness is hot
and in sporadic spaces
my mother praises, *You're so sharp!
Write a cover letter for your father.*
I draft her class reunion bio, compose witty
garage sale ads, pen congratulatory messages
in wedding cards, crack open my grandmother
Evelyn's eulogy, deliver and make
a million amends to anyone who ever worked
at or frequented a grocery store.

*I don't worry about you because you're not afraid
to speak up for yourself,* my dad says
to both me and my mother in a booth at a Chili's
after she expresses concern over my forever singleness.

His statement: true at a car dealership, on hold
with the home warranty company,
or at a protest is less so in quiet kitchen
moments with partners or parents
or my precarious mind,
always questioning what I'm becoming,
following me like some spirit that crept
out of a locker with a broken combination.

MY PARENTS ALMOST NAMED ME HEATHER, A GHAZAL

I'd have a medicine cabinet free of expired Advil, had my parents named me Heather.
She'd look smooth in bikinis, never regret her words. Sometimes, I'd rather be Heather,

paying housekeepers to mop her floor, flying first class to Turks and Caicos.
Dancing elegant salsa, unlike me, all bounce and wobble, she's carefree Heather.

Persuasive, long-necked, and knowledgeable about cryptocurrency.
The one at the tapas bar to figure out the bill, *yes we agree Heather*.

Pushing her cart past the bakery's lemon ricotta cookies, escaping to kale aisle,
weighing herself each morning, netting daily losses, see Heather's

thin thighs, perfect eyebrows, minimalist apartment, books organized by color.
A volume of Shakespeare's collected works, thoroughly read. *Gee Heather,*

where do you find time? her friends ask, *You're so different from Valerie, so put together.*
She answers, *it's all in my name, bitches, behold queen bee Heather.*

A CHERRY THAT CHOKES

I grew up in a narrow ranch house set
on a flat, two-acre square within the empty rectangle
of North Dakota. Our backyard lined with a thicket
of chokecherry shrubs. A windbreak of wild green
guardians that, like a cheap window, permitted
all the snowy prairie gusts entry.

During summer, the chokecherry shrubs bloomed
white flowers, which turned into crimson berries. A surprise
to my eight-year-old eyes—this hadn't happened
since the year before.

By late August, red berries ripened brown.
My mother and I picked chokecherries, plopped
them into buckets, popped them in our mouths, anticipating
strawberry shortcake. A jelly donut in fruit form.
Instead I pucker my cheeks, wish I could spit them out.
A first lesson in lowering expectations.

They whispered to my tastebuds,
try one more; maybe they'll get better.
The cigarette of fruit.

A different August, maybe I am ten,
I gobble a handful of tart marbles.
Let them roll on my tongue.
The skin sticks to the inside of my cheeks.
I swallow the fruit, left with a mouth
full of pits and the mystery of how to dispose them.
My teeth coated in dark chocolate. If dark chocolate
tasted like dirt. I remember:
I hate chokecherries.
But every late summer, I'd eat them,
again and again.
Maybe this time it would be different,
the addiction of rationalization.

My mother grew up on a farm in the 1960s. Candy and treats
were sparse, so the annual chokecherry harvest was Woodstock.
We didn't know any better, she tells me.

When I visit North Dakota, I shop for a gift
for my house sitter. The small boutique, empty
except for rows of chokecherry jams and syrups. Defeated
labels on the bottles, as if they've accepted, *we know
we only taste good when you drown us in sugar.*
A healing chokecherry tea to make one want to stay sick.
Chokecherries fermented into wine
to help one forget they're consuming chokecherries.

A hard fruit from a hard place.
It can be eaten.
Its Missouri River sunsets can be enjoyed.
But it takes effort,
tablespoons of sweetener.
Snowblowers pushed for blocks.
Abdomens wrapped in layers of fleece,
wool, coated in nylon.
Heads turned the other way when reading
their neighbors' political yard signs. I left
because I know better. To me, North Dakota
is a bitter berry.

PART III
FULL-FAT CAPPUCCINO

THE RED HOT DOGS FROM NORTH DAKOTA

Before I put my phone in airplane
mode, my mother texts,
You know, they're sold

at Seattle Mariners games,
always reminding me of my home
state's claims to fame: low

living costs, Lawrence Welk, liberty
of unlocked doors. Sameness
equals safety.

My mother
did not know what a Seattle Mariner
 was until the baseball team

started selling Cloverdale
Meat's fuchsia franks, a cheerleader
for locally manufactured mishmash.

To me,
the map to my origin
is mile-marked with monotony,

summer concerts in wheat fields,
bonfire blonds drinking
pro-life pilsners to death.

The same local cheerleaders
I could never pyramid.
But my mother and I,

we are both
romantics.
She wraps

herself in a fuzzy comforter
of familiarity.
I drool

on Delta fleece,
then text selfies 4,800
miles away,

biting into a spicy mustard
street wienerwurst under a
neon-

lit midnight, standing sandwiched
between an art gallery and
neo-renaissance opera house

commissioned by a 19th century
emperor in Vienna, the city
that rebirthed hot dogs.

IN PARIS, WHERE EVEN WORK IS ROMANTIC

The puppet man enters the subway,
erects a pole, hangs a curtain,
pushes play on his phone.
Opera pours out his Bluetooth speaker
as the train pulls away from Arts et Métiers.
He ducks behind the curtain,
a voyeur,
as the wooden suitor awakens
and professes
love to his mistress timed
out precisely: two minutes,
forty-six seconds of efficient romance.
Leaving him twenty-eight seconds
to collect coins from the car's other morning commuters
on their way to the cubicles and hard hats
and shared workspaces and garbage trucks
that they hide behind to make a buck.

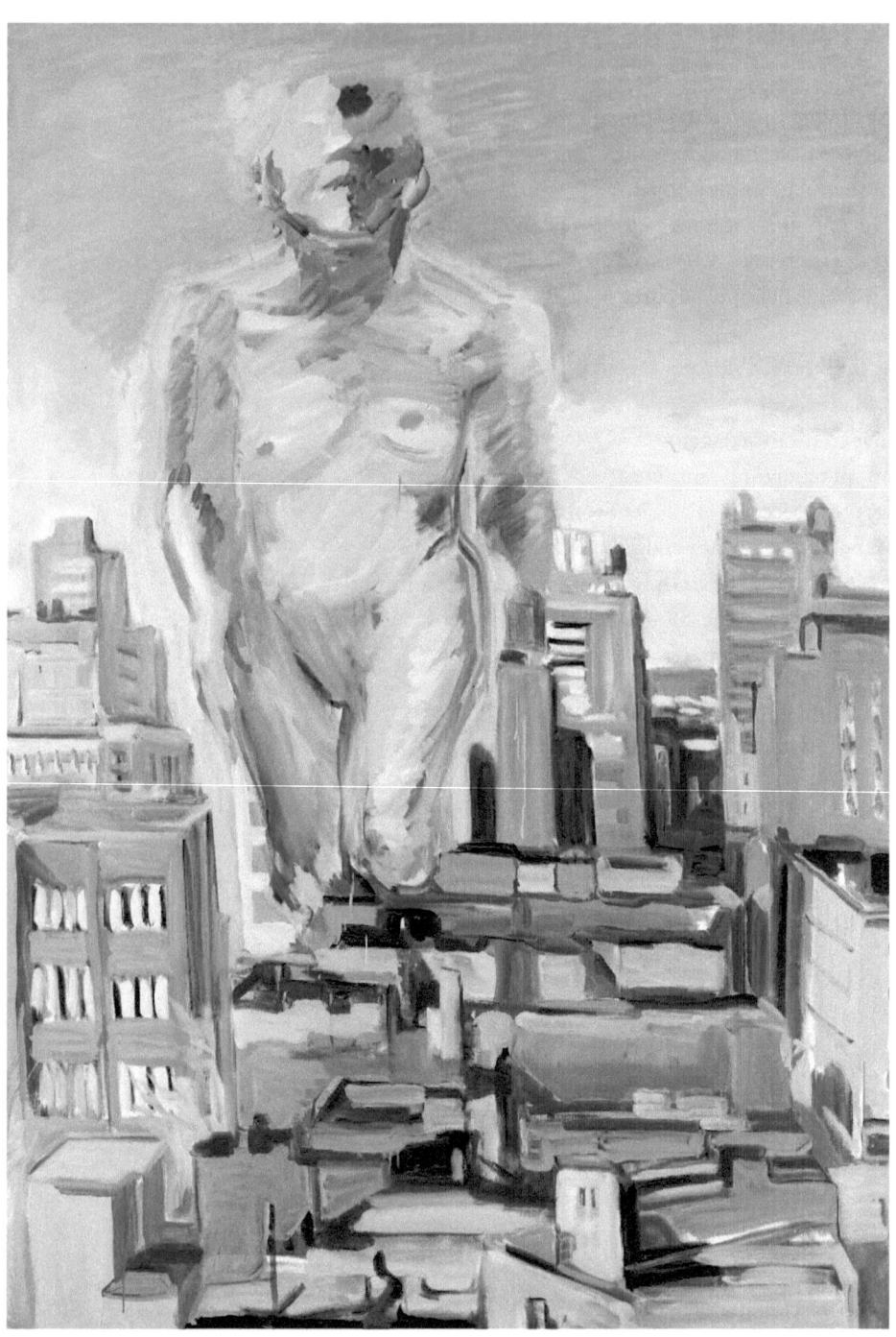

Maria Lassnig, *Woman Power*, 1979
© Maria Lassnig Foundation
Courtesy of The ESSL Collection (photo: Graphisches Atelier Neumann, Vienna)

ODE TO WOMAN POWER, A PAINTING BY AUSTRIAN ARTIST MARIA LASSNIG, WHO GREW INTO NEW YORK CITY CIRCA 1979

She grows taller than the Chrysler Building,
surpasses glass ceilings,
skyscrapes her head
on sunrises,
stomps concrete, leans
on a city that celebrates
inspiring,
statuesque, artsy
ladies.

A city
so big she can
be naked-on-the-subway
authentic. Towers of freedom
from hairstyle anxiety,
from uneven breasts,
from thigh potholes,
from a Rikers Island
of body insecurities.

Where she gives purpose
to pastel perpendicular
streets right-angled
into avenues. Where her art
shapes the square grid
of Alphabet City.

View painting here:

ATTEMPTING TO ACCELERATE PROGRESS

Barefoot men zig-zag their motorbikes, stacked five feet tall
with bundled ranunculus, crates of peonies and sturdy lilies,
weaving between stalls of carnations, daisies, buckets of sunflowers propped
on short, primary-colored plastic stools, winding
between laborers, exhausted roses yelling in Vietnamese,
between Western tourists watching petaled pollution

through their phones, between vendors haggling over bouquets
for restaurants and hotels and street selling
fragrant capitalism. It's 11 p.m. when Hanoi's
Quang Ba flower market opens.
I pick a lotus, vibrant pink, closed like a bird's beak.
I want it to open before we depart Hanoi for Danang
in a few days. The woman who sells it to me suggests
adding warm water to the vase each morning
to encourage the flower's opening.
*That's all it takes? Here, I've spent seven
years in therapy, still closed,* I say.
She doesn't laugh,
because self-deprecation doesn't translate.

After I return from my trip,
my relationship ends. I sit in an office
in Austin, Texas, Googling *how long*

does it take to get over your ex? over and over— I
read every book about attachment theory,
talk to five psychics, an energy healer, an evolutionary astrologer,

the seven-year therapist. I take ecstatic dance classes and wake up early
to run because it's the only thing that might pull the pain from my core.
It works, but only for a few minutes, so I supplement with screaming.

I write a letter to my mother, forgiving
her for things she doesn't know she did, but never send it.
I write a one-woman show, and people actually pay to see it.

I do *The Artist's Way*, and I'm not even embarrassed.
I write a letter to my inner child,
which feels so silly, but the energy healer
emphasizes as the most important step.
When I was in Hanoi,
I never saw the lotus open.

Instead, the warm water trick deepened half-opened
petals from pink to purple,
then let them drop.

FOUR ENLIGHTENED AMERICANS TRAVEL TO ANTIGUA, GUATEMALA TO BUILD A HOUSE AND VISIT RUINS

Rickety sidewalks
ensure we walk
                        slanted   wary of our steps
                                                              and staph
                                                                 infections.

The buses: late.

No one wears a watch.
Two men   repair   a single pothole in a cobblestone road   by
      hand over the course of two weeks   with one shovel
            and a single axe.

Hilltop villages built from Ozarka plastic bottles and Domino's pizza
boxes. One-room houses with a hole in the middle of a concrete floor to
piss in. When not in use, covered with a teapot lid.
And everyone smiles.

Our laundry is handwashed crisp.
Fresher than it's ever been.
We haggle in markets over pennies
for handmade handbags we'd spend dollars and dollars and dollars
for in any U.S. zip code.
The coffee wakes us like the
clouds of black exhaust booming from the tail pipes
of shiny turquoise and red chicken buses,
salsa dancing with the scent of melons and pineapple
orchids and bougainvillea,
honeyed mangoes.
Pleasant pollution.
For we are eennliightened amiricaaans, the New Zealander
says over Gallo beers and flaming shots of la cucaracha.
Salut!
And the pretty, petite Guatemalan girls sing songs.
And the men all over give us Spanish lessons,
and now it's time to get back on the plane,
back to Prozac smiles and honeyed

frowns, back to
Dallas,
back to rushed
hours, and the bus is
late again.

MATES VERSUS MATES

Available, feminist, spiritual, financially responsible, intellectually curious...
To the men I date, my list of prerequisites for a mate (American definition)
is as long as the Sandstone Peak in the Santa Monica Mountains
is tall. The same mountain I pointed to while hiking
with my available, feminist, spiritual, financially responsible,
intellectually curious friend Juani and asked her,
What's that one's name?
Straight-faced, she said, *Benjamin.*

After our hike, we spent seven hours
at Point Dume, beach blanket-dining on chicken salad
with homemade mayo and babble-singing
our gratitude for the Malibu sunset like only
close pals can: *Mabiboo. Madibababoo.*
The platonic version of obnoxious PDA.

My list of prerequisites for a mate (British definition)
is as short as the chorus to Natalie Cole's "Wild Women
Do and They Don't Regret It"—which Juani not only watched me
belt out, as we drug our sandy feet back to her Fiat after the tangerine sky
said goodnight, but joined in and recorded so I could post
to my Instagram followers—
someone who can fill a canyon with conversation.

THE PRIVILEGE OF NEVER HAVING TO GO HOME

It's Thanksgiving 2016, and I'm flying back to North Dakota,
because when I bought the ticket in October, Hillary was winning.
Beside me in 17B, a Mexican woman named Gloria in her sixties,
or an un-sunscreened fifties, hugged inside a deep pink winter coat,
clasps the handle of her lap's carry-on baggage, tight, like mothers hold
babies or daughters hold guilt.

Her fingers, plump as pillows but hardened
like worn down feathers. We speak in broken
versions of each other's languages. She's from Guadalajara,
returning to her job at Cloverdale Meats, the plant near my hometown
that processes premium pork products.
Gloria says she only sees her family

once every few years. I think this is sad, but maybe she too has a
complicated relationship with her place of origin. A fuselage of sorrow
barrels through the sky somewhere between Dallas and Bismarck,
so one of us can desert her loved ones to slice Thanksgiving hams
that will be placed at the center of tables in D. R. Horton-manufactured
dining rooms while the other takes bites to avoid arguments

about inequalities that float beneath polite conversation
like grease from breakfast bacon.

AN ENDLESS DRIVING SESTINA
after Miller Williams

Between Austin and Taos, miles of antique shops and banners for trump.
Can you even imagine four more years of this? Fuck
I thought there were more of us than them,
but you wouldn't know it by all these billboards for guns,
or I guess it's a pizza place named Six-Shooter. How strange is west Texas?
It's still two hours to Lubbock? I swear you said that two hours ago, my god

you could fit Ireland inside Texas nine times, god
this state is huge. Truck stops with lone star flags trumpeting
you're here still, in the big ego state of Texas.
Wind machines resemble seagulls. In Malibu, I once saw two seagulls fuck.
It didn't look fun for the female, a quiet assault, a mugging without guns.
Fields of oil rigs, dinosaurs bobbing, slurping juice from dinosaurs and

a wide sky of giant clouds that proclaim we create presidents and
Miss Americas and angry, italicized billboards advertising a God
who blesses fetuses but not children, and the limitless number of guns
one can legally open-carry in Texas. Laws on track to trump
Gilead's. Fuck
Texas.

Some say the Balcones fault line is the beginning of west Texas,
or maybe it's where billboards advertise faith over fear and
confederate flags wave in yards to remind neighbors of fears. Fuck.
Maybe it's where cotton fields wind forever through so much, god
damn Texas. Obnoxiously large, a blaring trumpet,
mandating longer waits to get an abortion than to buy a murder of guns.

Maybe it starts after another shooting, where even an El Paso Walmart protests guns.
So much has changed in four years, even my Facebook feed persuades a purple Texas,
but out here in Coleman and Santa Anna and Lubbock, trump
banners are as popular as taxidermy and
BBQ. Only god
knows what will happen, what did happen. Why ignorance wins. What the fuck?

Fuck
guns,
God,
west Texas, and
trump.

Eventually it ends. West Texas,
it does. All it takes is driving twelve hours, a border crossing, and
desert scarce hope to stop seeing signs for trump.

TRAVELING DURING A GLOBAL PANDEMIC

Ten months of Sundays, I circle my neighborhood.
The chatty brook in the greenbelt
across from my apartment now transformed
into the Trevi Fountain, surrounded by prickly
western horsenettle shrubs, quieter
than tourists. Their yellow berries, poisonous
like iPhones in front of faces.

I stroll down an alley imagining
it's a gelato shop. Peruse rainbow rows
of modern condos painted pistachio, hazelnut,
accented with splashy mango, strawberry-sorbetto
front doors. Each agave plant, a statue
of a Roman emperor. Each driveway with a parked Acura,
a thrift store bragging vintage Prada in the window.
Every abandoned mask on the sidewalk, an orphaned
Italian leather glove on cobblestone.

I've memorized every terracotta planter,
every local brown-and-white mutt,
every no-longer-surprising speed bump,
like a tour guide knows each of the
Colosseum's 80 arches.

I bump into the old ginger cat from the
white brick ranch house four blocks away who runs
toward me. Maybe we're on the Spanish Steps. Strangers flirting
like Gregory Peck and Audrey Hepburn.
If we squint,
perhaps this could all be a movie.
A temporary holiday.

MEXICO CITY IS SINKING

The uniformed men playing
organ grinders in her historic center
hold out their tan hats for tips
in front of her blue and white house
of cracked ceramic tiles, slanted floors and rocky
foundations, playing whiny music
no one asked for. I walk
like a cautious hen on uneven sidewalks.
I've fallen in many cities, and I can't stop
looking at the exposed tree roots, lifting up asphalt
like botanical Hercules.

In my hotel I read about urban forestry
while eating chicharrones marinated in Valentina
and lime juice, a hot warning in my mouth.
It's because of earthquakes, the experts say
in a scientific paper from 1986, that's why the city
is strangled in tree roots. I'm no scientist. I prefer
to think in myths. Maybe the city got too cocky.
Now as karmic punishment, she sinks twenty inches a year.

I mean the Aztecs built a city on mush
after the universe told them to. After they asked
the gods for a sign undeniable.
*Show us an eagle eating a rattlesnake
on top of a cactus.* It sounds ridiculous, but I too
have read a horoscope, asked the universe
to bless me in feathers, to tell me I am loved.
Reaching all the time upward is exhausting
and maybe it's easier to lean into Mictlan.

Mexico City is sinking, like all the coolest swamp
towns, smelling vaguely of shit, sewage stewing
barely beneath cobblestone.
Venice's columned palaces shrink
under sea tapestries. The Atlantic can't wait to swallow
Miami's art deco goddesses. New Orleans, a bowl
of hurricaned magnolias.

It's hard not to judge history's fools.
Why erect a home on waves?
But I too have built a grand thing on mud,
have a hard time letting go of a bad idea.

PART IV

100-CALORIE PACK

SNACKS FOR THE LOVE HUNGRY

When I say *monogamy,* you sink
like undercooked quiche. Your sea-
salt-flecked stubble scratches my chin raw
all night as we negotiate whether to have sex.

The next morning, we share brownies. No man
has ever baked to woo me, and I am starved. Predict
the taste of chocolate before
the experience unfolds on my tongue.

Because you quote Esther Perel with a British accent,
I believe you'll be good to my heart. We sizzle
through a fall and winter. You ask if you can make me,
your *girlfriend,*

saffron risotto. I say *yes! Of course.*
You ask if I have saffron.
I say
yes,

of course.
You put me to task,
stirring arborio rice in a cast iron skillet.
Grains stick to the pan's bottom.

The heat's too high.
You hold me the night before my birthday. A treat
that only happens now after you return
from some place hours ahead, Moscow, Cardiff.

Can you tell from the future what becomes of us?
I wake up to homemade coffee cake. I dislike
it, but eat the whole
loaf. Safe and comfortable

with things that no longer bring pleasure.
A warm avocado and zucchini salad served
on a summer evening. Frida Kahlo made
it for Diego Rivera, you foreshadow. We eat dinner sitting on your slippery

leather couch, a middle course between watching an HBO drama
and another midnight bedroom talk, peppered
with passive aggression: to stay, I have to over and over
again bring the main ingredient. To stay,

you have to empty your surplus for a woman, ravenous.
Toward the end,
I buy those soothing synthetic
cucumber eye patches, found on endcaps

of the serpentine checkout at Marshalls,
like bakers stockpiling pantry staples,
and, for months, cry to a feast of friends
in Magnolia Cafe over buttery pancakes,

slices of blueberry pie,
gallons of decaffeinated grief—
solo *traveler* twirling a fork of cacio e pepe at an osteria in
Rome, eager inner *child* scooping

Hanoi's spicy beef and papaya salad into her mouth,
curious *wanderer* eating street-
grilled lobster beside an island
mutt named Kaya—

the meatiest life
I've savored,
I dined on
without you.

FIVE STAGES OF GRIEF

ONE
My car dies. I ask you to bring tacos. You tell me *it's too rainy to drive*. I lie. Say *that's fine*.

TWO
I pick up your Levi's off the bedroom floor while you shower.
Insert my left leg in your jeans, then my right, sneaking closeness you've stopped giving.

THREE
I brag to coworkers when you buy me roses,
but all I wanted was your presence, not an apology bouquet.
Honestly, a box of Kleenex would have been more useful.

FOUR
The bed where we argue is eerie.
Like the Marfa lights, I'm never certain
if what I see is really there,
or if I want a story to tell my friends.

FIVE
I grip a stubbled No. 2 pencil, circling
answers to a quiz in a self-help
book about attachment and intimacy,
answering questions as if I were you.
Then again, as if I were the you I wished you'd be.

IF I'D PUT MY CLOTHES BACK ON AND LEFT YOUR BEDROOM

when you told me you never intended to remarry,
I'd already have been a healthy woman. But no one delights

in eating kale, and your bed was an arcade
of white linen denial where, every night, I played pinball.

But let's say I was a person
who made rational decisions while half-naked,

a woman with a PhD in acceptance,
a Buddhist nun who identifies songbirds

not with an app but with her third eye chakra,
who goes to bed by 10 p.m. and sleeps the entire night.

A sage who never spent three weeks addicted
to Candy Crush, who takes the vitamins

lined up in bottles on her kitchen counter, who drinks gallons
of restorative holy basil tea, who runs marathons

because she enjoys long-distance pain. Imagine
running for pleasure instead of away from fears

so big they could fill the entire 1,800 acres of the San Diego Zoo—
a sanctuary, a prison, or a whimsical field trip destination where children

gawk at the orangutan notorious for escaping
cages. What if I were a life coach

with an actual life others want,
or a sensible woman who plays backgammon?

Or maybe a goddess with a mind quiet, amused
by reading a book or, God forbid, even writing one.

If I'd put my clothes back on and left your bedroom
that day, folded my hands in puritanical

prayer, nothing rich could have followed.
Sometimes a novelist throws out 500,000 words,

starts over, and at first that seems like despair.
But one hundred and fifty years after a publisher rejected

Louisa May Alcott's *Little Women*,
Greta Gerwig turned it into a film,

which I watched in a theater alone while eating popped
kernels of newfound singleness,

because watching movies solo
is a thing one does while working on herself.

And you and I, we got a story.
No one talks about that publisher except for writers.

No one talks about the part
we call working on ourselves.

ODE TO DEWALT

It's true, my workaholic father did not
equip me with a secure attachment
style. But he did buy me
every possible power
tool to prepare
me for years
of fixing
myself.

12 MOURNING HABITS FOR A PRODUCTIVE SORROW

1. Do not make your bed. Open a notebook. Write down one question: *When will this end?*
2. Forget to pray.
3. Strap on your sneakers for a quick jog into the abyss. If no nearby abyss, try a ravine.
4. Once arrived, scream at rocks. Scare a fox. Sing yourself a lullaby. Take a nap on the bank of a river's end.
5. Wake up, stomp back home. Assign meaning to every stray feather you see on sidewalks. God is a ginger cat who murders pigeons.
6. Eat a plate of cold spaghetti noodles, best slurped in your unmade bed.
7. Hold an unopened meditation book and cry. Or don't, and wonder why you can't.
8. Imagine drinking vodka. Or gasoline and lighting a match.
9. Stretch yourself into staring at your phone for undetermined amounts of time.
10. Dehydrate. Birth a three-day headache.
11. Contemplate what it would feel like to feel a body on yours without feeling.
12. Sleep with your best friend. Or a stranger. Neither will damage you as you find your way back to your insides.

HANGING YOUR NAME ON THE WALL

Maybe it was our tenth date. We mixed
low brow with high: cheeseburgers and an art gallery.
Some women, when they make love,
withdraw from their own pleasure
to appear sexy for a man.
I don't do that in bed, but to the detriment
of my own enjoyment,
I did try too hard
to look adorable,
seated across from you while eating
delicate bites of a Shackburger.

Later at the gallery, a woman
wearing leopard-print loafers compliments
my color-blocked outfit: gold corduroy skirt,
burnt-orange tights, red suede boots. Your face
reads her praise
as a five-star Yelp review.
Neither she nor you know I bought
ten skirts after our first date just to prove
I was enough.

You linger
in front of an exhibit—used envelopes covered
in black ink drawings of human silhouettes—
the first time you say my name to me.
Valerie, see this?
You point at these unassuming
common objects elevated into art.
Oh, wow, Jim. I echo.

Saying each other's names feels
like speaking a new language for the first time.
Like we got caught talking shit. Except
we were gossiping to each other.
Not like how it feels now to say your name.
To my therapist. Over and over.
Or defensive when I say it to my mother.
Or like when I say it to Tessa, every Saturday morning on the trail,
trying to sound aloof.
It feels different from how it sounds now,
in a poem about you. A name I would never
choose to put in a poem:
Jim.
Unsophisticated.

One syllable.
Kind of a stupid name.
The name of a man you call to find out if you qualify
to refinance. A Jim sells tires,
or helps you change one, without instilling fear.

It is not the name of a person exalted
into ubiquity like *Starry Night* coffee tumblers
the entire population of everywhere seems to carry.
Not the name of a person whose memory hangs
out for seasons like an abandoned
wasp's nest under an awning.

SINGLE WOMEN CAN'T STOP BUYING SHIT

If everyone were in a healthy relationship,
there would be no marathon runners,
no chopped bangs,
no aisle of memoirs.
Iceland's tourism would sink
without newly single women
hoping to solo trip their grooves back.
Poor Taylor Swift would be poor.
Like mosquitos and cockroaches,
heartbreak is a necessary nuisance.

AN ALGORITHM OF IMAGINED FUTURE HORRORS

I am married
to my fears of your future rebound,
committed to the cloud of women
who post laughing face emojis
on your unfunny Instagram posts.
Mainly puns.

I can't blame them for digital flirtation.
I too laughed harder at your jokes than they deserved,
obsessed over your beach photos.
Now I'm jealous of a feed
of exotic women: Ilise who bakes French pastries,
funky-earrings Inez from Colombia,
Danica who makes candles in North
Carolina,
Lilli, doppelganger for Phoebe Waller Bridges,
Sophie: polyamorous belly dancer.

Sirens you give attention
to because they are safe zeroes and ones.
Women who I predict will do what I could
not:
open your emotional unavailability.

I build an imaginary algorithm of future horrors.
Women who are not humans, only reasons
why I wasn't good enough.

When we started dating
you introduced me to the Instagram account @thingsorganizedneatly.
Images of office supplies arranged by color.
fall flowers lined up by height like an elementary
school group photo. When I scroll through it now,
I still find the images satisfying: OCD-grouped cookware,
Roy G. Biv-sorted cell phones, and I envy you.

Drawers of avoidance that easily slide shut,
a love fit for The Container Store.

But my emotions spill like overturned
couch cushions in a movie-scene burgled apartment.
I hold them simultaneously: rage and longing
and sometimes something near grace,
while I imagine you've filed us
between almost and fear,
between healthier than your ex-wife but more challenging
than the common Jessica who keeps liking your posts
of pineapple-garnished cocktails
and self-deprecating dying cacti.
A notary public with a lithe dancer's body
and large forehead. A puritan who,
unlike me, would never dare ask to
meet your parents on Thanksgiving,
let alone share on your second date
that she has to order a steak because of her heavy
period anemia.
No,
this woman is tidy and easy
and organized neatly.

With a feed consisting of simple Midwestern meals,
perfectly placed plates of spaghetti squash,
crockpot casseroles, and 16-ounce glasses of milk.

Like the post of ombre slices of toast,
you arrange each of your emotions with precision,
compartmentalize them in a library card catalog,
so intimacy and anger and vulnerability
never meet.

NOCTURNAL INTERSECTION

Last night, I dreamt I sat on a bus,
across the aisle, one seat behind you.
We were no longer
together. I inhaled tears
to hide that you once meant something to me.

Passengers on our way to different futures.
Or at least, I got off at the Galleria in Houston.
When I walked through Nordstrom's doors it turned
into a gift shop in Taos, New Mexico. I exhaled tears inside the store.
A sales lady asked me to sanitize my hands with a bottle of popcorn oil.

Last night, you dreamt we were together
inside a Blockbuster, feeling guilty about not supporting Vulcan
Video but how could we? We were in Houston, not Austin.
I told you I never liked pinball, which you heard with your chest.
It sounded like rabbits hopping inside your lungs
while a train sped through your brain, back and forth
between your ears. We couldn't decide on a movie,
rented a bottle of Tom Ford's Oud Minérale cologne,
got on a bus. I sat across the aisle, one seat behind you
in my own dream. I left, and you wished you had something to watch.

A GOLDEN SHOVEL FOR A WIDOWER NAMED WAX
after Gwendolyn Brooks

How many poems will I write about the times we
walked around urban lakes, bragging about our real

connection because we share a birthday, *how cool
is that?* you keep saying over and over, like somehow we

traversed the cosmos, ran red lights through lifetimes, took a left
turn at the sign for soulmates and settled in to school

each other on emotional availability and electronic dance music. *We
only live five minutes apart*, you say. *Why don't we hang out more?* You lurk

in persuasion, pressuring me to replace your boredom, your loneliness, your late
wife who you say you're over because you're not the one who died. *We

were about to have a baby. I was about to be a dad. Strike
that.* You latch onto my eyes, wishing they were a uterus delivered straight

to your door like an Amazon package. You claim you're not clingy. *We
both like Szechuan string beans.* You turn this non-thing into another sign, sing

the NPR programs we have in common. I laugh and you act like that's a sin.
We are nineties kids who listen to KCRW, we are two adults who claim to like art, we

are white people who eat pasta and talk about climate change while jazz
plays in your dining room for a few evenings over the course of a few weeks in June

and July in the strange part of a pandemic where we aren't certain if it's over and we
don't know what comes after the ampersand and we can't figure out why we didn't die

and why so many others? And why *she* did too soon.

IN CARE OF LALO

Loving him was like eating key lime pie
for breakfast, lunch, and dinner,
while having a diabetic foot amputated.
His Chilean accent and midnight overtures blinded
me from his monobrow and unavailability.
He was a plate of cacio e pepe from the coziest
osteria in Trastevere, that is, if the silky
noodles were peppered with rat poison.

Lalo, a man who danced kizomba—
stand-up sex—with a shibari knot
of exotic flamingo women who were not me,
the woman he said he loved most.

I was a feral kitten starving for milk,
my head trapped in an empty jar.
In this scenario, Lalo is the jar.
He is also the one who rescued me from the jar
by extricating himself from commitment,
allowing me to find a future worth biting.

But how could I bite back, Lalo?
Give him an unfulfilling gift of
subtle revenge?
Perhaps he thinks of me
when opening his overstuffed
mailbox filled with too much,
which he claimed I was. AARP offers,
glossy L.L Bean catalogs, boxes of Omaha steaks,
mealy golden pears UPS'd from a Harry & David
warehouse, penis enlargement pills, aquamarine
advertisements for Disney Cruises with obnoxious mice,
flyers for mail-order brides,
in care of one Lalo Banks Alvarez.

PART V

TRAIL MIX

A PLEA FROM THE POET'S UNOPENED MAIL

I am patience manifested,
so damn good at sitting still

with Capital One credit card applications
and a Design Toscano catalog,

selling ornate Victorian thrones and medieval dragon sculptures
as if you live in a castle and not a womb-sized condo

with limited closet space and a dining room table constructed
of unopened mail. I am a stack of nagging

mothers lecturing you to take action.
I am the NAACP and Planned Parenthood and ACLU calling

you to renew either good personhood or shitty selfishness.
Hanging onto the weekly circular from the grocery store

you don't even shop at, and what kind of privileged
person are you if you don't use coupons?

But it's not like you're a total mess.
If you were, Discover

wouldn't offer you pink credit cards with 0 percent APR.
But you could be better.

Perhaps if you subscribed to Purple Carrot's vegan meal prep,
you'd function as a self-actualized adult.

A postcard from the Turquoise Trader where you once bought
a white buffalo ring you love but can no longer find

because you live in clutter.
Bleached business envelopes loiter before your front door.

An unwelcome
mat. Evidence of decision paralysis.

Remember when your boyfriend dropped
by and you hid me with a blanket? And then he left anyway?

I beg you to stop hiding.
Stop using me as a curfew of shame.

You could trash me entirely.
That's fine!

Or smooth slit each envelope open
with a butter knife and dare to see the contents inside,

which could be terrifying but might be easier
than you think. Might be everything you need.

Like a supplied
postage paid reply envelope.

IT TOOK ME 39 YEARS

Some babies belt out affirmations
as their mothers push them through the womb
and grow up feeling worthy.
I spent a Tae Bo teenagehood
figuring out the best way to shrink
my thighs in the dryer. Ran a track
of laps in my twenties
and wore Forever 21 flare skirts
to distract from my meaty quadriceps.

Appreciating myself is something I schedule
two alerts in my phone to remind
me to do, and then ignore.
Loving my thighs, crafty tongue, too-short
frame, imperfect impulsivity, hairy vulva,
my belly where English toffee and dark chocolate
built a sprawling suburban mall,
my fear, my me-ness never came naturally.

It's easier to do pilates and 21-day fitness
and blame the patriarchy and measure quarter cups
of high-protein, low-fat Greek yogurt
and wear shoes that fuck up my feet
to make me two inches taller.
If loving thighs were chess,
scolding them while wearing
a one-piece swimsuit
is tic-tac-toe.

I'm the only person I ever needed to cover
a mirror in Post-it notes to trick
myself into loving. My insides crave a tyrant.
It only took 39 years and hearing a man
for whom I offered too much of my love
to tell me he loved my thighs. His validation
is all it took for me to permit myself to remove
the Post-its so I could admire my own damn legs.

And for that, I hate myself.

EARTH HAS ATTACHMENT ISSUES

During its infancy Earth wasn't held

for as long as it needed by the Milky Way.

I mean it wasn't anybody's fault.

The galaxy has 500 billion celestial bodies

to tend to, wailing for milk.

Perhaps if Earth were hugged

by rings like Saturn, or if God

hadn't walked out, or it had not suffered

from effects of solar nebula postpartum depression,

we inhabitants would float untethered.

But Earth has attachment issues, love-crave clinginess

so encompassing that it uses gravity to latch

the boots of 28 billion human feet to its surface, root

three trillion trees to its core, dock maritime vessels

to ports, bathtub shelter two-ton blue whales,

draw dragonflies to meadows, seduce city sky

-scrapers, captivate crickets, attract apples

to the ground, enchant everyone to stay a little longer,

planted in bed, hit snooze, snuggle, more

please, play hooky, roll beneath the covers

like meteorites tumbling

their way home.

TO THE PROFESSOR WHO FIRST ASSIGNED ME J. ALFRED PRUFROCK

I was 18, too high, wearing ill-fitting thrift store corduroys.
She was dressed in L.L. Bean, the kind of quiet
that commands attention. A queen with an empire-sized
knowledge of British literature.

Who taught *Walden Pond*, but openly laughed
at Henry David Thoreau's privilege. Who made Mary Wollstonecraft
interesting. Who was out in a town
where no one was out. Who joined the Peace Corps,
rode motor scooters in Cambodia,
birdwatched.

Who was good at doing things people who live in North Dakota
don't do while still adoring North Dakota, which I could never do.
Who complimented my sardonic eyebrow. Who I now see on Facebook,
retired, posting travel photos. Who I eat lunch with on visits
back to my hometown. Who doesn't like spicy food.

She traveled to Austin once. I picked her up from her hotel,
took her to the Mayfield Preserve, a botanical garden where dozens
of beautiful peafowl wander, fanning tails under willow trees.
Peacocks nesting in live oaks, albino ones prancing across a
swampy southern path.

We walked twenty feet into the park, where she wanted to sit
on a bench and chat about imposter syndrome. I told her I got sober
and procrastinate too much at work. She said everyone wastes
time on the job, even deans, and shared how odd
it felt when she noticed the lightness
of her keychain after she retired.

She pointed to a white-winged
dove pecking at the ground. The whole time, she didn't say a syllable
about my impressive peacocks.
White-winged doves are like pecan trees in Central Texas.
Everywhere. Boring. I hear them every morning.
Except I never realized I did, until chatting

with my professor 1,500 miles away from where I first
met her twenty years ago. I always wanted poetry to be
Paris and peacocks. But it happens on park benches
and in coffee spoons.

SOMETHING THAT MAKES HIS VOICE CREAK

I think love is against me, but with every returned box
of toiletries, I build an Eiffel Tower from self-help books—
and isn't growth the most loyal paramour?

Derek Thomas, the nerdy sixth grader who could have been my
first clumsy kiss, but who I swore off because he bent on one knee
during recess. He grew up to be a securely attached
Audi owner. Instead, I kissed no one until I was drunk at 15
in a hotel room with a college-aged boy whose name is listed
in the blackout pages. A spiced rum adolescence.

I can't stand how many valet drivers
I've fallen for who discovered a new way to pronounce
Nietzsche instead of learning to identify
an emotion. I'm not blaming these guys.
Although without alcohol,
my only high left is blame.

I want to know more than a man's
Wi-Fi password, more than the radio stations
programmed in his car, more than the steps he choreographs to dance
out of relationship. Something I can't find online, something
that makes his voice creak. I want someone who risks

softness, which I myself have been practicing
now for at least a day.

A NIGHT SHIFT WORKER TO THE POET

I'm a guardian of night,
a blue-collar pillow,
absorbing each day's stress,
protecting enamel,
often stranded on the nightstand
coated in dried saliva, resting
in the valley between alarm clock and daily
meditations, ignored
for 16 hours, watching
piles of unfolded clothes grow
like well-managed 401Ks
and sansevieria waiting
for life to begin,
or at least a water break.

Later, I'm brushed with paste, shoved
inside my cave of purpose, a buffer to
prevent teeth grinding on teeth.
But my work doesn't matter
because the tension
still exists. Like the hostility
I feel toward sleep mask,
who does nothing but lie there all night
or the envy I feel toward melatonin,
who delights in the easy work of dreams.

If I could give her one piece of advice,
I'd tell her to relax.
But then I'd be out of a job.
And then what?

HAIKU TO MY IMAGINARY FRIEND MARC MARON

Tender interviews,
extemporaneous truth,
honest guitar riffs.

In the beginning,
I listen to whining rants
because I relate.

It's 2012.
The year I stop drinking booze,
you are a fellow.

Happy-hour headphones,
playing WTF,
one day at a time.

We have in common
sobriety and coffee,
comedy and cats.

Brimming with anger
fear and jealousy toward
one Louis C.K.

You disarm each guest
with one simple inquiry:
What does your dad do?

Farmed and factoried
and cleaned. Fixed all things broken.
I'd share this with you.

Expect us to laugh.
Two people who talk too much,
in need of repair.

MY FRENEMY, THE SUPER PLUS TAMPON

Like a girl from high school with whom one shares
an eating disorder and a zip code,
we bonded out of necessity.

Vanilla cheerleader transformed into wavy redhead.
In only 1.5 hours. My period, prompt like a junior
league teatime ritual. Dense scones soaking
up pools of clotted cream.

Chumming around, codependent.
You only adored me when I was dizzy and
weak. I used you. Gave you (and your 35
friends) purpose. A monthly hazing.

The reason you found your way into my late 30s
ended up being the cause of our eventual rift:
anemia induced by orange-sized, eggplant-shaped unnecessary
tissue, a fruit basket of fibroids, pressing, pushing, bullying
the parts of me that never became anything.
The become-less, mopped up with your necessary tissue.

Blood sisters.
Pacts between you and me—between
my uterus and a future version of me I never made—
babble-language translator, tuition saver, curfew enforcer—
broken.

After kicking my uterus out of the clique,
I dug out the extras of you from my bathroom cabinet,
handed them to every woman I ever met.
A period Santa Claus.

Now when I push
my cart through Target on my way to buy cotton
balls and conditioner, I ignore your aisle. Pretend
not to see you, not to remember my lost
sorority membership card.

WHAT I REALLY HEAR WHEN HE SAYS WE ARE "JUST HANGING OUT"

We are not dating / but also, might be characters in the first act of any Jane Austen romance / He never healed from his third-grade teacher calling him ugly / A stroll around a farmer's market where he buys Thai chilis, and I'm sold a basket of future dinner assumptions / An ex-girlfriend, thinner and less whiny about the patriarchy, hides in the backseat of his brain / This is the reason I learned so much about Bukowski in dorms when I was 21 / A Rorschach test / The reason I apply Russian Red lipstick before leaving my house, but then mute it with Cool Girl Pink before he answers his door / I never healed from my mother doling out love lopsided, like unmixed chocolate chip cookie dough / An almost-welcome mat lawn of plush green fleece fortressed by an invisible fence / The reason I learned so much about Jim Jarmusch in coffee shops when I was 31 / The sound of a slot machine that always lands on two cherries and one marriage proposal / Reason enough to walk away

HENRY WINKLER GIVES ME PERMISSION TO QUIT THERAPY

The actor who played *Happy Days*' Arthur Fonzarelli picks me
up. Holds me, fatherly. In fact, he's a giant.
We're approximately 1300 feet up in the sky looking down
at the Chrysler Building.

I'm so afraid of heights,
I don't even drive on flyovers, erupt into panic attacks
looking at friends' Costa Rica jungle vacation zipline photos.
I don't know where the trauma
originated.

I suggested Midtown Manhattan
because If I'm going to hyperventilate
in midair, at least give me something gorgeous
to meditate on

beyond flocks of geese and airplane contrails.
We admire the art deco building's ribbed sunburst crown,
a rust-proof ornate steel helmet
for 77 floors of concrete.

Winkler leans on the delicate but durable
spire with his elbow.
Tells me he believes in therapy,
then gives me permission to quit.

*A person can sit on a couch and yammer on about relationships
for eight years but at some point, she has to take off her protective
leather jacket and get out in the elements.*

I listen while counting eagle gargoyles jutting out from the 61st floor
(a somatic exercise my therapist suggested).
Eight aerodynamic guards
watch over this Manhattan gemstone.

*A black leather jacket is a classic, but don't forget
about amber and gray and camel suede,* Winkler says

I squint and ask him to bend down, so I can see the riveted
hubcaps adorning the building's 31st floor exterior.
He scoops me in one hand, lowers me.

If you're scared of letting go
of your therapist, remember there are always
other therapists. Or acupuncture. Or Judaism.

He continues telling me about how his father, who survived
the Holocaust, smuggled the Winkler family jewels
out of Germany by covering
them in melted chocolate, then carried
a box of chocolates in his hands,
passing through border crossings,
declaring he had nothing valuable to Nazis.

The things we use to hide value
can sometimes become the value, he says.
Like a story about tenacity and survival
lasting longer than family heirlooms.
Or a hubcap accessorizing
a wheel while keeping out debris.
One day, who knows,
you could build
a skyscraper outta that thing.

MY IMMUNE SYSTEM IGNITES A FOREST FIRE ON MY SKIN, AKA A PANDEMIC PANTOUM

My skin itches.
I'm allergic to my mask.
The agony of safety.
What next?

I'm allergic to my mask
on a third date during a pandemic.
What next?
How are we gonna kiss?

On a third date during a pandemic.
This country is so dangerous.
How are we gonna kiss
without some sort of commitment to work toward?

This country is so dangerous.
We're all gonna die anyway
without some sort of commitment to work toward
a secure future.

We're all gonna die anyway.
So who needs mouth monogamy
for a secure future?
The only thing scarier than a pandemic is intimacy.

So who needs mouth monogamy?
The agony of safety.
The only thing scarier than a pandemic is intimacy.
My skin itches.

Listen to poem here:

A DAY'S WORTH OF NET LOSSES & GAINS, APRIL 16, 2021

Losses:
Cheek collagen, unknown amount.
2.75 hours of sleep to thoughts about mopping my kitchen floor.
935 American lives to COVID-19.
The will to broil a salmon fillet.
The ability to remember the word *synchronous* while on a work Zoom.
A morning workout.

> Gains:
> A productive morning writing session.
> An oat milk latte from Café Crème.
> Annoyance from the maskless man sitting inside Café Crème.
> The sight of two red-wing blackbirds
>   perched on a bay laurel tree in Mabel Davis Park.
> My mother calling to say she found
>   a seven-layer bar recipe that calls for coconut oil instead of butter.
> Text endorphins from a salt-and-pepper Hinge stranger named Luke.

Loss:
A future with Luke because he neglected to ask me a single question.

Gains:
Time to myself.
Self-respect.
Serotonin from black rice horchata coconut milk ice cream (substitute for
    both dairy and love).
Answers to questions I imagine Luke could have asked: fresh-cut flowers,
    hammocks, watching sunrises in foreign countries, 8:17 a.m., Sharon Olds,
    integrity, three to four nights a week.

> > Loss:
> > Someone to sit beside me on this goddamn couch.

Gain:
Serenity.

LAST NIGHT, MY POTHOS PLANT

dreamt
it was in a movie
with Helen Mirren who played a therapist.
For once, the plant was happy
to be sitting in a chaise lounge in the center
of the room instead of by a window
on a ledge, eavesdropping.
Pleased to answer questions about its mother,
instead of listening to me talk
to myself. Then the plant ran
a bath. Because it was a dream, the tub
was the kind with claw feet. The bathroom, the size
of a grand Italian villa. Instead of water,
Neem oil dripped from the faucet into the white
porcelain tub. What a relief!
The pothos has been stressed
and suffered from an infestation of those little no-name
black flies. My pothos plant dreamt my gray tabby,
who diurnally sticks his wet pink nose in its leaves,
somersaulted into a powdery bath bomb,
disintegrated upon hitting the water in the tub.
Then the sun whispered
its alarm through the sheer curtains
and woke the pothos. It's still
adjusting since humans shortened the
nights.

FIRST DATE WITH HERMAN MELVILLE REINCARNATED

So intimate with Ishmael and Bartleby,
he must have been Herman Melville
reincarnated. Character analysis, plot,
symbolism—so enamored with his own voice,
so adamant about the
single
right
answer.
All I wanted
was to wander around words
and split a slice of cheesecake.
So when he asked
if I wanted to go out again,
I told him
I'd prefer not to.

THE SPIGOT FAIRY

My neighbor has her groceries delivered but is too drunk to put them inside.
Two paper bags, two bottles of champagne bubble in her entryway.
Four boxes of Franzia at the front door.
I haven't seen Drunk Debbie sober in ten years.
It's been five years since I saw her stand straight.
In blackouts, she takes my neighbors'
Amazon packages and tears down
UPS notifications taped to our doors.

One time in the parking lot, she stumbled,
crying. I helped her up. Cheap wine
floating from her pores.
She told me her wrists were weak.
That's why she fell.

I remember, every winter before a forecasted freeze,
for years, our outdoor spigots
would be covered in Styrofoam caps to protect the pipes.
We always thought it was the property management,
but turns out, it was Drunk Debbie,
the spigot fairy.

When I first moved to Timber Ridge, Drunk Debbie
used to hang out on the front lawn, bitching about the HOA.
But she wasn't yet Drunk Debbie. She was
Always-Inviting-Me-To-Drink-Red-Wine-On-Her-Porch Debbie,
which I declined because I was
Drink-Solo-On-My-Own-Porch Valerie
until that one final drunk dial, one final
leaving the front door open all night
when woke I up and surrendered
myself to seltzer water.

It's been at least five years since Drunk Debbie stopped taking care of our spigots.
I rarely have to avoid her when I see her outside,
wobbling around the mailboxes, while I shake my head, *tsk, tsk,*
what a shame. Like she isn't who I was drinking
my way toward becoming:
the well-intentioned woman alone
in an apartment with her champagne shades pulled down,
toasting to smallness
because it isn't dark or pathetic or insane
if it pops fancy flowing over a flute.

TO THE MAN I DATED WHO THOUGHT SUNSETS WERE OVERRATED

I say *whaaa? Are you KIDDING me?*
You must live in a topsy turvy world where *overrated*
means *Holy Hell this is a Wild Cotton Candy Lava Lamp* haloed

above my head. You're telling me your sad-belly
Netflix-scrolling existence isn't entranced
in envy by the way the sky dragqueens

tangerine and periwinkle on her eyelids? EVERY TWELVE HOURS
(give or take depending on how close to the equator).
She's such a hit with audiences,

the universe gave her an eternity-long residency.
She's the muse for Cirque du Soleil, soufflé, and Monet.
And that's just in France.

The inspiration for Barbie's Dream House, frozen yogurt parfaits,
yacht rock, My Little Ponies, steel pedal guitars,
Icy Hot, mango sticky rice, Morgan Freeman's voice,

Lisa Frank, terracotta pots, fairy godmothers,
blueberry cobbler, stucco-climbing bougainvillea, beaches
on every continent, the city of Venice.

My girl delights the planet
daily, and you are not moved? There's nothing
I could do, no perfectly poached pecan-crusted

salmon I could cook, no sexual technique I could thrust
upon you, no conversation witty enough.
You are unimpressed by the most impressive

and I'd rather be alone.
But I'm not, because every day I notice and thank my treasure,
my love, who paints her adoration for me across the sky,

and because I forget I am worth it
she makes sure to do it twice.

HAPPY MEAL HOURS

Like me, the McDonald's Happy Meal was invented in 1979, so I have a soul
connection to a box of junk endorphins, learned young to reach for dopamine
hits: sugar, salt, fat, tiny toys, miniature Muppet Baby Fozzie Bear,
a personified McNugget pirate, layers of loaded marketing.

Plastic playthings inside placentas of plastic to protect them from runaway
fries and me from my Rhea the bully reality and innate inadequacy.
An origami box folded into golden arches of love.

Happy Meals were the origins of my bliss point entitlement
that evolved into happy hours, that, like Jesus, turned
water into wine, I turned into nine,
into closing time. Pints of time spent imagining
happiness with friends and then serotonin strangers
I imagined were friends.
Are you happy? my mother asks
at the end of a phone conversation
where she questions my drinking.

I lie but don't know I'm lying.
Say *yes, I'm happy*. But every morning, I zombie
commute, hungover, fantasizing a life in an exposed
brick apartment in New York. A Netflix comedy special, a cat
who doesn't wake me up. If I had a Vitamix, I'd be happy.
Or a mother who understands me.
When I find a guy who sticks, I'll be happy.

Everyone has a reckoning.
McDonald's started offering apple slices
and milk. I traded in dive bars for
church basements. I'm still uncertain I've experienced happiness.
Perhaps, when I stopped
envisioning exposed brick.

THE WHITE PICKET PROMISE

My upstairs neighbor
wakes me up at 2
a.m. with loud bites
of blueberry pie.

Each morning, she empties her dishwasher,
clanking stacks of boyfriends
into cabinets, banging
trust funds into the silverware drawer.

On weekends, she overfills her washing machine
with loads of collagen, creaks her bed
with airline tickets to Cabo,
throws dice of confidence

across her ceramic-tiled floor,
spends afternoons slamming
Jenga blocks of tequila,
and at 9 p.m. every night jazzercises.

Each jump an exclamation point
urging me to find a real estate agent.
To sell my 800-square-foot central Austin
condo that, like a mini skirt,

I've outmatured. Spent a decade surrounded
on three sides in this starter nook
near comedy clubs and coffee shops
and city center camaraderie,

building equity in future wife-ness
only to one day upgrade to a bigger shell
with a yard of my own to park my plants
and bury my anxiety.

But I've spent decades sprinting
away from shared Costco memberships
and split mortgages, so I might as well
compost courage in the suburbs solo.

Push a lawnmower across my own
cacophony. Repair a roof with my own
hammer, hang a hammock for one,
and fulfill the white picket promise myself.

ACKNOWLEDGMENTS

Some of the poems in this book were published in the following places. I'm grateful to the editors.

Bette Midler Dispenses Stray Advice During a Playground Game of Red Rover – Hash Journal

Burnt Honey – Anti-Heroin Chic

Collecting Cash at the Phallic Factory – Sand Hills Literary

Despairathon – Abandon Journal

Earth Has Attachment Issues – Sky Island Journal

Eddie Vedder Saved Me from a Cult – Olney Magazine

An Endless Driving Sestina – Oddball Magazine

First Date with Herman Melville Reincarnated – Rue Scribe

A Golden Shovel for a Guy Named Wax – Moonstone

Graduating from Sundaes – SOFTBLOW

The God Grid Failed Texas – Anti-Heroin Chic

Hanging Your Name on the Wall – Disquiet Arts

He Asks About My Kinks – Rattle

Henry Winkler Gives Me Permission to Quit Therapy – FreezeRay

In this House – SOFTBLOW

Late Stage Abyss Abecedarian – SOFTBLOW

Mexico City is Sinking – SOFTBLOW

My Frenemy, the Super Plus Tampon – Gnashing Teeth Publishing

My Immune System Ignites a Forest Fire on My Skin, aka a Pandemic Pantoum – Pine Hills Review

Ode to a Mansplainer – Drunk Monkeys

Recollections from the Poet's Training Bra – Disquiet Arts

The Red Hotdogs from North Dakota – Olney Magazine

Remnants on the Pool Table's Soft Felt – Anti-Heroin Chic

Spigot Fairy – Whiskey Tit

Zillow > For Sale > Late 20th Century Redhead – Jupiter Review

With thanks to everyone who has read my work in varying stages, especially Dena Afrasiabi, Christina Brown, Cassie Lewis, Raquel Luciano, and Melissa Sussens. Deep appreciation for Hiram Sims and Community Literature Initiative for bringing writers together and for helping me stay accountable. Extra high-fives to the Season 8 Monday night all-stars, Camari Hawkins, the Season 9 Thursday crew, and Carlos Ornelas.

My head bows in gratitude for my teachers and mentors, especially Megan Falley, and the entire Poems That Don't Suck community, Brendan Constantine, Sean Hanrahan, Elijah Pringle, and early cheerleaders Janelle Masters and David Pink (RIP).

Thank you to the global pandemic. Yes, that bitch who took away life as we knew it, but also gifted me the time to create my own version of a poetry MFA.

Lastly, a wicker basket of love and gratitude to my family, friends, sisters, and readers.

ABOUT THE AUTHOR

Valerie Nies is a poet, comedy writer, and gluten enthusiast who grew up eating carbohydrates on the plains of North Dakota. She is the author of the poetry chapbook *Imaginary Frenemies*. In her free time, she peruses WebMD, loses pairs of sunglasses at record rates, and wonders if the next man she talks to might turn into her next romance, or at least introduce her to a tasty new snack. She lives (and eats carbohydrates) in Austin, Texas, with her gray tabby Henry.

valerienies.com

www.ingramcontent.com/pod-product-compliance
Lightning Source LLC
Chambersburg PA
CBHW060532080526
44586CB00012B/706